We Are
The Dreams of Our Ancestors

Imani Brown-Ajayi, Mariama Dibba,
Dazariah Ellis, Nalah Fearce, Nandi Mawusi,
Wisdom Mawusi & Dr. Artika R. Tyner

Text Copyright © 2024 Planting People Growing Justice

Illustrations and Design by Reyhana Ismail at Rey of Light Design

All rights reserved.

No part of this book may be reproduced in any manner without express written consent of the publisher, except in the case of brief excerpts in critical reviews and articles.

All inquiries or sales request should be addressed to:

Planting People Growing Justice Press
P.O. Box 131894
Saint Paul, MN 55113
www.ppgjli.org

Printed in China
First Edition

LCCN: 2023935096
1-9781959223832-03/21/2024

Dedications

Imani Brown-Ajayi:
For my beloved mother, Ashlee Brown, and my grandmother, Daphne Brown.

Mariama Dibba:
For my caring family—Mommy, Daddy, Fata, Alajie, Seray, Coumba, Grandma Coumba, Grandpa Ibou, and Aja.

Dazariah Ellis:
To all the kids out there who want to change the world!

Nalah Fearce:
This one is for the Black babies.

Nandi Mawusi:
For my siblings who inspire me.

Wisdom Mawusi:
For my three divine Black, Bold, and Brilliant children who so generously share me with our community. Asante sana!

Dr. Artika R. Tyner:
For Dr. W.E.B. Dubois who inspired me to imagine, create, and build a better future.

We are regal,

Black and Brown —

From peanut butter to pecan,

We shine like gold in the sun.

We are many people built by tribes, cultures, and religions.

But that does not mean that we treat anyone differently.

We are human. We belong and deserve to be treated equally.

We are powerfully poised for greatness.

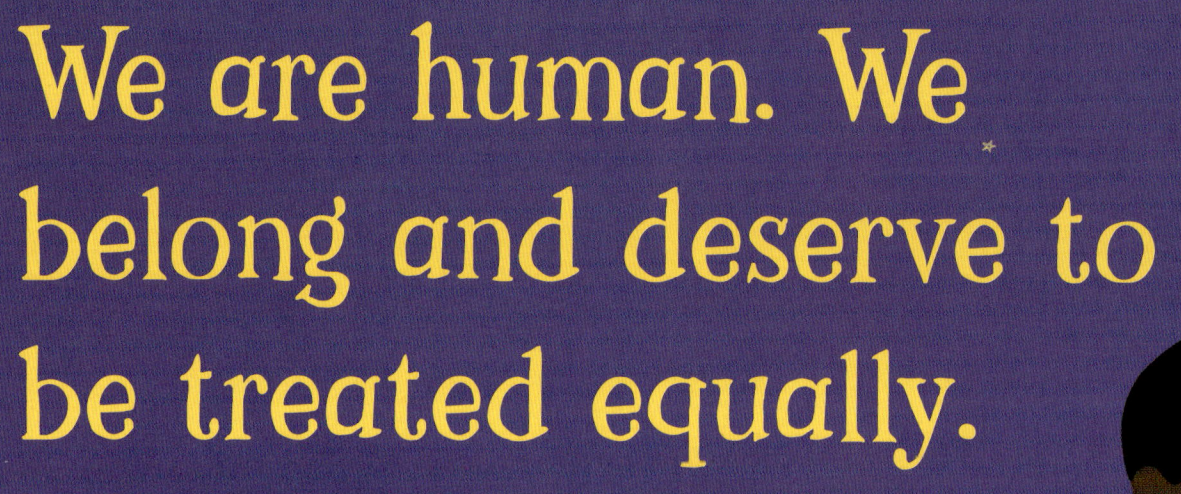

We are Black, Bold, and Brilliant, Rich beyond measure.

We are still here.

We are dreams being made true.

We are the courage and faith of our elders.

We are bricks together, not easily moved.

We are the foundation. We build the roots for each other to grow from.

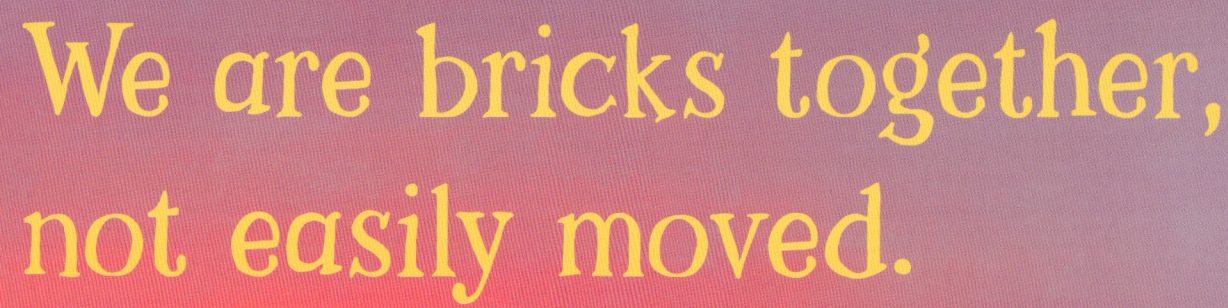

HARRIET TUBMAN	ETHEL WATERS	MADAM C.J. WALKER	BESSIE COLEMAN	ANGELA DAVIS	HUEY P. NEWTON	PAUL ROBESON
W.E.B. DU BOIS	FRITZ POLLARD	ALVIN AILEY	FANNIE LOU HAMER	BAYARD RUSTIN	FREDERICK DOUGLASS	ETHEL L. PAYNE	ROSA PARKS
JOHNSON H. JOHNSON	OPAL TOMETI	CARTER G. WOODSON	MAYA ANGELOU	PATRISSE CULLORS	JESSE JACKSON	MARSHA P. JOHNSON
MARIA P. WILLIAMS	WALLY AMOS	MAE JEMISON	SOJOURNER TRUTH	BARACK OBAMA	DOROTHY HEIGHT	NELSON MANDELA
MALCOLM X	ELLA BAKER	DON CORNELIUS	ROBERT SENGSTACKE ABBOTT	REBECCA LEE CRUMPLER	GORDON PARKS	THURGOOD MARSHALL
RUBY BRIDGES	IDA B. WELLS	SHIRLEY CHISHOLM	MAX ROBINSON	MARCUS GARVEY	JESSE OWENS	MARTIN LUTHER KING JR.
CLAUDETTE COLVIN	ANNIE TURNBO MALONE	ALICE COACHMAN	JAMES BALDWIN	HENRIETTA LACKS	ALICIA GARZA	SISTER ROSETTA THARPE

We bloom from within.

We are like rushing wind.

We are the hopes of our ancestors—

generations of strength, courage, and power.

Imagine going on a treasure hunt without a map. Would it be easy to find the treasure? Most likely not. Life is the same way. Without history and heritage, we would not know where we come from. History and heritage are like a map that can lead us to treasure. All we have to do is follow the path made by the people who have lived before us. Their lives show us how we can make the world a better place for everyone.

These "We are" statements tell stories of those who have lived before us. They also show us how we can be better each day. These statements teach us that our differences make us strong. They remind us that we are important and can help change the world. It is a good thing when we look at where everything started. This helps us see how far we have come. These statements show that we have come a long way and can go even farther.

Here are some ways to celebrate culture and heritage:
- Learn more about your family history.
- Interview a grandparent or community elder.
- Read about your cultural history.
- Participate in a cultural celebration like Juneteenth or Kwanzaa.

Majeste Phillip

Majeste Phillip is a passion-filled creative, striving to utilize her writing talents to challenge and inspire the world. She is currently pursuing her own pathway to law and justice working for the State of Minnesota and plans to continue her education in law school.

Websites

African American History at a Glance
kids.britannica.com/kids/article/African-American-history-at-a-glance/623342

Celebrating Black Leaders
pbs.org/parents/black-history-month

Discover the North Star!
nmaahc.si.edu/learn/digital-learning/north-star

Books

Charles, Tami. All Because You Matter. Orchard Books, 2020.

Joy, Angela. Black Is a Rainbow Color. Roaring Brook Press, 2020

Woodson, Jacqueline. This Is the Rope: A Story from the Great Migration. Puffin Books, 2017

ABOUT THE AUTHORS

Imani Brown-Ajayi

Imani Brown-Ajay is in the seventh grade. She lives in Minneapolis with her family.

Mariama Dibba

Mariama Dibba is a U.S.-born Senegalese-Gambian who embraces her culture, traditions, and Islamic faith. Mariama loves baking, reading, writing, and watching classic Disney movies.

Dazariah Ellis

Dazariah is an intelligent fifth grader who comes from strong, Black-empowered roots and was always told that she can change things. She attended Maxfield and lives in St. Paul.

Nalah Fearce

Nalah is from North Minneapolis. She is seventeen years old and is very passionate about art and activism and what they can create when they are put together.

Nandi Mawusi

Nandi is a vibrant, brilliant, outspoken and compassionate eight-year-old Black child. She resides in North Minneapolis with her family and credits them for inspiring her to write.

Wisdom Mawusi

Wisdom Mawusi is a writer, educator, activist and the mother of three divine Black children. She resides in North Minneapolis and is the founder and executive director of Black, Bold & Brilliant, an empowering community organization for Black youth and families.

Dr. Artika R. Tyner

Dr. Artika R. Tyner is a passionate educator, an award-winning author, a civil rights attorney, a sought-after speaker, and an advocate for justice who is committed to helping children discover their leadership potential and serve as change agents in the global community.

About Planting People Growing Justice Leadership Institute

Planting People Growing Justice Leadership Institute seeks to plant seeds of social change through education, training, and community outreach.

All proceeds from this book will support the educational programming of the Planting People Growing Justice Leadership Institute

Learn more at www.ppgjli.org